30 Days with Mary

You can read more about Emily and her
books at:
facebook.com/profile.
php?id=100005373166724&fref=ts
or
twitter.com/EmilyOwenAuthor

30 Days with Mary

A devotional journey with the mother of Jesus

Emily Owen

Authentic

First published in 2014 by Authentic Media Limited
PO Box 6326, Bletchley, Milton Keynes, MK1 9GG.
authenticmedia.co.uk

British Library Cataloguing in Publication Data
A catalogue record for this book is available from the British Library
ISBN: 978-1-86024-935-8   978-1-78078-255-3 (e-book)

Cover design by David McNeill revocreative.co.uk

for my mum

Philippians 1:3

Acknowledgements

Thank you to my parents. You have been unfailing in your spiritual, emotional and practical support and I am so grateful for you both.

Thanks to the team at Authentic Media, your guidance has been invaluable.

Many thanks to Robin for getting me started on this journey.

As ever, thank you to my Heavenly Father – to him be all the glory.

Introduction

What must it have been like to be Mary, the mother of the Son of God?

Take a look at her diary, sharing in her trials, her excitements, her fears and her joys.

As you read it, you can learn from Mary, be challenged by her, grow closer to Jesus with her . . .

Each day's reading ends with 'Mary's Memo'. This is a challenge to keep in mind throughout the day and to be remembered when situations happen or people cross your path.

The 'my response' bit that follows is for you to use in any way you'd like. Maybe to record thoughts, feelings, actions or aims that have stemmed from the day's reading.

It is worth pointing out that while most of the diary entries are based on biblical fact, a few times it was necessary to 'fill in the gaps' – I did this by researching what life was like at the time and by trying to put myself in Mary's place (I have been a teenaged girl!).

Please do read the biblical accounts, particularly in the books of Matthew and Luke, from which I gathered the information for Mary's diary. Remember that anything not found written in these accounts is conjecture.

Introduction

It is my prayer that reading Mary's diary will challenge and encourage you in your Christian walk and will draw you closer to Jesus.

Emily

See, your Saviour comes . . .

Isaiah 62:11

Day 1

I have decided to keep a diary about my life.
My name is Mary.
I am 14 years old.
I live in Nazareth.
I have brown hair.
I like cooking.
I don't like doing laundry.
My favourite colour is blue.

Imagine you have decided to keep a diary about you
and your life.

What would you write on the first page?
What do you think is important about you?
What would you change about yourself?

When other people look at you and your life,
what would they think your priorities are?

Now, imagine God has decided to keep a diary about
you and your life.

What would he write on the first page?
What does he think is important about you?

What would he change about you?
When God looks at you and your life, what would he
want your priorities to be?

Now compare the two sets of answers.
How are they the same?
How are they different?
How do they challenge you?

It has been said that God loves you just the way you are,
but he loves you too much to let you stay that way.

Let's take that in two sections:

'God loves you just the way you are . . .'

God loves you!
Isn't that amazing?
The God who created the universe loves you.
Because you are you.
Even though you're not perfect.
Even though you get your priorities wrong.

God loves you, just the way you are.

Why not remind yourself of that as you go through today?

When things go well – coffee with a friend, a hug from a
child, an unexpected phone call – say to yourself,
'God loves me.'

And when things don't go so well – you snap at the kids, other road users drive you mad, there's a massive queue in the supermarket – say to yourself,
'God loves me.'

'. . . but he loves you too much to let you stay that way.'

Because he loves you so much,
God wants to mould you.
To change you.
To make you more like Jesus.

2 Corinthians 3:18:
'We . . . are being transformed into his likeness.'

Are you letting God transform you?

You could start by praying the prayer below, based on Ephesians 3:17,18.

Lord God,

I pray that, as I make this journey with Mary, I will understand, more and more,
just how wide and long and high and deep your love for me really is.
And I pray that I will allow it to make me more like Jesus.

Amen

Mary's memo

God loves me

My response:

Day 2

I'm so excited! I've wanted something like this to happen for so long, and now it has! I can hardly believe how it happened, though, so I'd better start at the beginning.

It was my turn to go to the market today, so I set off quite early in the morning. It's great when it's my turn to go; I love getting away from the house for a bit.

Anyway, I did the shopping and set off for home. I had to walk past the synagogue on my way and, just as I passed the entrance, I tripped on a loose stone. My shopping went flying, fruit and vegetables everywhere! I was really embarrassed and hoped no one had noticed but, of course, they had. And it wasn't just anyone, it was Joseph. He's the man I've had my eye on for ages. And there he was, picking up my shopping and helping me up. I tell you, I wanted the ground to open up and swallow me! Talk about making an impression. I couldn't even meet his eye, just muttered a quick 'thank you' and hurried home.

But he's so nice! The way he helped me, didn't make a fuss, just got on with it. And he's easily the best looking man there, and the kindest. Oh, I can't stop thinking about him!

When was the last time you couldn't stop thinking about someone? Or something?

Maybe you can't stop thinking about your endless 'to-do' list, or what you can't eat because you're on a certain diet, or the holiday you're planning with your friends, or the new clothes you need to buy for the kids, or even something more serious, like an illness or a hospital appointment.

Now, ask yourself, when was the last time you couldn't stop thinking about what you'd been reading in your Bible, or what you'd heard in the sermon last Sunday?

When was the last time you couldn't stop thinking about God?

If it was a while ago, if you've lost your joy in the Lord, why do you think that is?

Perhaps it's other things getting in the way,
life becoming busy . . .

If you've lost that joy, how can you get it back again? How can you restore your relationship with God?

Psalm 23:1–3:
'The LORD . . . leads me beside quiet waters, he restores my soul.'

There are no short cuts – if you want the joy, you need to start at the beginning.
If you want your tired soul restoring to joy, you need to allow yourself to be led beside quiet waters.

Which will probably mean slowing down sometimes.
Taking a break sometimes.
Saying 'no' sometimes.
So that you can say 'yes' to taking time out with God while he restores your soul.

Restores your energy, your excitement,
your enthusiasm for him.

Restores your joy.

So you can say with Hannah (1 Samuel 2:1):
'My heart rejoices in the Lord'.

Lord God,

I have lost some of my joy.
My joy in you.
And I want it back. I need it back.
Please help me.
Help me to take time to be led by you beside quiet waters.
Time to let you restore my soul.
Time to let you restore my joy.

Amen

Mary's memo

Rejoice!

My response:

Day 3

Oh my goodness. Joseph turned up at our house this evening. He wanted to check that I was OK. Then he had a chat with Dad and, to cut a long story short, Joseph and I are engaged to be married. This is what I've been waiting for; this is where I belong!

Where do you belong?
Not what bank do you belong to, or what gym, or what library.
Where do you as a person belong?

Or, to put it another way;
Where do you feel accepted?
Where do you feel wanted?
Where do you feel valued?

Mary would probably have felt these things when she became engaged to Joseph. He wanted her, he valued her, he'd chosen her as his bride and he was going to marry her.

Colossians 3:12 refers to,
'God's chosen people . . . dearly loved'.

Think about it;

Chosen.
Accepted.
Wanted.
Valued.

Now think about the identity of 'God's chosen people'.

Well, one of them is you!

Accepted, wanted, chosen, valued by God . . . you.

Let's look at a parable Jesus told (Matthew 13:45,46):

It is about a merchant.
A merchant who is looking for something.
He is looking for pearls.
And not just any pearls; the pearls he is looking for have to be the best.
So he looks and looks . . . and eventually he finds one.
He finds the pearl he's been looking for.

But it's expensive. Very expensive.

What to do?
Maybe it's best to just forget about the pearl?
After all, he has many other treasures at home.

But no – this pearl is special.
So the merchant goes home, sells everything he owns, comes back and buys that pearl.

Did you notice something in this story?
The pearl did not do anything!
The merchant wanted the pearl just because it was a pearl.

God accepts, wants, chooses, values you . . . just because you are you.

It's true, he does!
But maybe it makes you uncomfortable?
Makes you think, 'Why would God accept, want, choose, value me?'

The answer is – because he loves you.

Personalize 1 John 3:1:

'How great is the love the Father has lavished on [me], that [I] should be called [a child] of God! And that is what [I am]!'

Lord God,

I'm amazed that you want me,
that you love me,
that you choose me,
that you value me.
But thank you that you do.

Amen

Mary's memo

I'm chosen

My response:

Day 4

Well, today is the first day of my life as an engaged woman! As soon as I woke up this morning, my first thought was, 'I am going to marry Joseph,' and then I just lay there, daydreaming, until I heard Mum reminding me that it was time to get up. And that today is my turn do the laundry. I don't like doing the laundry, having to go out into the courtyard with all the other women and listen to them gossiping and bickering. But maybe it would be OK today. I'm the one that's got news for once.

So I carried the washing outside. Sure enough, there were a few women there already, so I hurried over to tell them about my engagement . . . but every time I opened my mouth, one of them interrupted. Someone's sister had had a baby, someone's brother had broken his leg, someone had had a bad sleep last night, someone wanted help with their housework . . . and on it went. I might as well have been invisible. No one was taking any notice of me. I was sidelined and I felt as though I would burst with frustration.

Have you ever felt sidelined?

Ignored?

Not listened to?
Maybe by friends, family, church?

Let's look at Luke 18:15–17:

Jesus was very popular. Everyone wanted to see him,
whether they liked him or not.

One day some people brought their children to Jesus.
They wanted Jesus to bless the children.
But, when Jesus' disciples saw them coming, they told
them off.
They told them to go away.
They sidelined them.
The disciples thought that Jesus wouldn't be interested
in children . . .
and they were wrong.
Jesus called the children to him.
And he welcomed them, each and every one.

In yesterday's passage from 1 John, we focused on the
first part of the verse.
Now let's focus on the second:

'How great is the love the Father has lavished on [me],
that [I] should be called [a child] of God! And that is
what [I am]!'

What does it mean to be a child?

Well, it probably means different things to different people but, for most children, it means to be dependent, to be reliant, to look to other people for help.

Now, remember that you are a child of God.

Do you depend on him, do you rely on him, do you look to him for help?
Or do you prefer to be an 'adult child' of God – his child in name but not in reality?
Not in a way that says, 'God, you have control of me. I'm dependent on you.'

It's hard to be God's adult child, isn't it?

It's good to be God's child child, isn't it?
Or don't you know the answer to that one?

If you've never tried it, why not try it today?

Hand things over to God.

Let him Father you.

Isaiah 40:11:
*'He gathers the lambs in his arms
and carries them close to his heart'.*

It's a great thing to be God's child, to remember that you don't have to go through things alone.
To remember that he is always there to help.

Lord God,

Sometimes I forget how to be a child.
I'm so busy being 'in control' that I forget that I don't have to handle everything by myself.
I forget that you want to help.
I do want to be your child again.
I want to rely on you and to remember that you always welcome me.
Please help me to start today.

Amen

Mary's memo

I'm God's Child

My response:

Day 5

Well, if yesterday turned out to be less exciting than expected, today was the other way round. In fact, I think today has to be one of the most surreal days of my life.

I was just looking after the animals. We had walked quite a long way to find better pasture so, when we did find some, I sat down in the shade. The day was hot and I fell into a doze . . . until I heard a voice saying, 'Greetings, you who are highly favoured, the Lord is with you.' I thought I must be dreaming, but the dream didn't go away. In fact, the more awake I became, the more real the 'dream' became. This may sound crazy, but the voice I'd heard belonged to an angel. And the angel was about 2 feet away from me. I was petrified and also worried – why was an angel bothering with me? I blinked hard and pinched myself a few times, just to be sure I wasn't imagining this, and I think the angel must have taken pity on me because he spoke again, 'Do not be afraid, Mary, you have found favour with God.'

The story of the angel Gabriel visiting Mary is very familiar. Sometimes, this familiarity can make it lose some of its impact.

So let's try to look at it through fresh eyes:

Mary is told that she is highly favoured,
that she has found favour with God.

Pause a minute . . .
Mary has found favour with God.

She doesn't appear to have done anything in particular
to have brought this on,
yet here is an angel telling her that she has found favour
with God.

How do you think that made her feel?
How would it make you feel?
To do nothing amazingly wonderful and yet to be told
that you have found favour with God, that you are
special to him?

In fact, let's re-phrase that question – how *does* it make
you feel?

Because God also says to you, 'You are highly
favoured.'

Personalize that:

'I am highly favoured.'

'God highly favours me.'

One definition of 'favoured' is 'to support, to root for'.

Just as Mary would be supported by God in all that lay ahead for her, so, too, God will support you in all that lies ahead for you, whatever that may be.

He'll support you, encourage you, strengthen you – he's rooting for you!

Isaiah 43:1,2,4:
'I have redeemed you . . . When you pass through the waters, I will be with you . . . you are precious and honoured in my sight, and . . . I love you'.

Lord God,

It's hard to believe that you highly favour me.
Help me to believe and accept that you do.
That you are supporting me,
encouraging me,
strengthening me.
Thank you that you are rooting for me.
Thank you that you think I am worth it.
Help me to remember that today.

Amen

Mary's memo

God's rooting for me

My response:

Day 6

It's me again. Still reeling with shock, to be honest. It's hard to believe an angel actually visited me. Anyway, this is what happened next . . .

The angel told me I'm going to have a baby! Yikes, I've only just got engaged.

There was the angel, telling me all about how great this baby would be, and there was me getting more and more confused . . . so in the end, I just asked him straight out. 'Hang on a minute,' I said. 'I'm a virgin, so how will all this stuff you're talking about possibly happen?'

Here we have a classic God perspective/human perspective clash.

God says, 'this is what will happen,' and we say, 'hang on a minute, what about x/y/z?'

One example of this kind of clash is found in 2 Kings 6:8–23:

Elisha's servant is panicking. His city is surrounded by the enemy army – every direction he looks in he sees enemy soldiers, horses, chariots.

So, he's panicking like mad and,
to make matters worse,
Elisha is just calmly sitting there, not saying anything.
In the end, it is too much for the servant . . .

He rushes over to Elisha and blurts out,
'This is a nightmare!
We're surrounded!
They're coming to get us!
What are we going to do?'

And Elisha replies, 'Don't worry.
There are more on our side than on theirs.'

Huh?!

The servant looks around and counts up the number on
their side . . . exactly none. Well, two, if you count him
and Elisha, but they're not really up for fighting.

The servant looks back at Elisha who, once again, is
sitting calmly, this time with his eyes closed.

Elisha is praying; 'Lord, open his eyes.'

And the Lord answers Elisha's prayer.

The Lord opens the servant's eyes and the servant sees
'the hills full of horses and chariots of fire all around
Elisha'.

The servant didn't realize it, but God had it sorted all the time!

What a great thing to remember – God's got it sorted.

Whatever it is, whatever happens today,
God's got it sorted.
His way.

The servant had his eyes opened and he saw things from God's perspective.

1 Samuel 16:7:
*'Man looks at the outward appearance, but the
Lord looks at the heart.'*

As you go through today, try to see people and situations as God sees them.
Try to look from his perspective.

Lord God,

*Thank you that you have everything sorted.
I don't need to panic.
Help me to put that into practice.
And Lord, give me eyes that see people and
circumstances from your perspective. Help me not
to base my opinions on outward appearances.*

Amen

Mary's memo

Lord, open my eyes

My response:

Day 7

Still trying to get my head round all this . . . the latest is that it's not just any baby. This baby will be great and will be called the Son of the Most High. What?! 'The Most High' must mean God, right? And get this, Elizabeth is pregnant! My cousin . . . surely she's too old to have a baby?

My head was spinning; I could feel a headache coming on. I had so many questions whizzing round –

What . . .? Why . . .? How . . .?

I think my confusion must have shown and the angel took pity on me again. He explained, 'Nothing is impossible with God.'

Nothing is impossible with God.

Or, to put it another way:
Everything is possible with God.

Do you believe that?
Really believe it?

Believe that God can deal with your confusion, failure,

temper,
disappointment,
fear,
anger,
things you keep buried and hidden from the world?

Let's take a look at Moses.

Moses was adopted.
Exodus 2:10: '[Moses was taken] to Pharaoh's daughter and he became her son.'

Born a Hebrew but raised as an Egyptian, Moses grew up feeling that he didn't quite belong.
Exodus 2:11: 'Moses . . . saw an Egyptian beating a Hebrew, one of his own people.'

Moses had a temper.
Exodus 2:12: 'Glancing this way and that and seeing no-one, [Moses] killed the Egyptian.'

Moses had a terrible secret.
Exodus 2:12: '[Moses hid the Egyptian] in the sand.'

When Pharaoh heard of this, he tried to kill Moses.

Moses was scared of other people.
Exodus 2:14: 'Moses was afraid and thought, "What I did must have become known." '

Moses ran away.
Exodus 2:15: 'Moses fled from Pharaoh'.

Moses was alone.
Exodus 2:15: '[Moses] went to live in Midian'.

When given a job by God, Moses lacked self-confidence.
Exodus 3:11: 'Who am I, that I should go . . .?'

Moses certainly had a lot to deal with.

Do any of his feelings ring true with you?

Now ask yourself, is Moses' personal CV one that would be at the top of the pile, or straight in the rejection bin?

Probably, humanly speaking, it would be in the bin but, heavenly speaking, it went straight to the top of the pile.

What made the difference?
Exodus 3:12:
'God said, "I will be with you". '

It's not a what, it's a who!
It's God.

God would be with him.

Day 7

And suddenly, Moses has the best CV for the job.
What's your personal CV like?

God says to you,

2 Corinthians 12:9:
'My grace is sufficient for you, for my power is made perfect in weakness.'

If you have God with you, you can deal with anything.

Lord God,

I do believe that you can deal with things that I keep hidden.
Help me to let you in.
And Lord, I often feel like a failure.
Thank you that your grace is sufficient.
Please perfect your power in my weaknesses.

Amen

Mary's memo

Nothing is
impossible with
God

My response:

Day 8

'Nothing is impossible with God.' OK, so there I was,
waiting for the next bit, but the angel just stopped
talking. There was this silence, which I knew I was
supposed to fill. He was waiting for me to speak.
Well, I know that God can do anything, I really
do, but I guess I've never really been faced with this
question before – do I want him to do what he wants
with me? I do in my head, of course I do, but now
we are talking about reality. And a very strange
reality at that. Having a baby was definitely not on
my immediate agenda. But it seems it's on God's
. . . me, God, me, God . . . it feels as though I'm
having a tug of war. I closed my eyes. The words
went through my mind faster and faster – me, God,
me, God . . . and suddenly I sat up straight. Of
course I have to do it God's way. If I don't, 'me and
God' will just come apart and I will drift away. I
couldn't stand that. I have to be with God, whatever
happens. So I opened my eyes and said to the angel,
'I'm God's. Let him have his way with me.'

Have you ever had a tug of war with God?

Maybe you're in the middle of one right now . . .

Let's look at Cain, Genesis 4:

One day, Cain and his brother, Abel, brought an offering to God.
Abel brought his best lambs, while Cain brought some of his crops.
We don't know what crops, but they were clearly not the best that he could bring.

And so the tug of war starts –

Cain wants to give to God, God wants Cain's best, Cain doesn't want to give his best . . .
a step away from God.

So, God is not pleased with Cain's offering in the way that he's pleased with Abel's, which makes Cain really angry . . .
another step away from God.

God comes to Cain and reassures him that he can still be accepted,
he can still get back on track . . .

But by now, it seems that Cain is even further from God.
He doesn't respond to God's offer of reconciliation at all, but chooses to go and kill his brother instead . . .
another step away from God.

Then, when challenged by God about the murder, he lies outright . . .

another step away from God.

And then God banishes him . . .

Do you see the downwards spiral?

And all because Cain tried to do it his way,
not God's way.

God always knows best and always wants the best for us.
But sometimes it can be easier to acknowledge in our
heads that he knows best, rather than in our hearts.

Jeremiah 29:11 (NLT):
' ". . I know the plans I have for you," says the LORD.
"They are plans for good and not for disaster, to
give you a future and a hope." '

Will you say with Mary, 'I'm God's. Let him have his way
with me'?

Lord God,

I do know that your way is best.
At least, I know it in my head.
Help me to know it in my heart.

Amen

Mary's memo

God knows best

My response:

Day 9

Came down to earth with a bump today. Was on such a high after meeting the angel and realizing that God truly does know best. But today I remembered that this is not just about me. This involves Joseph, too. How am I supposed to tell him that I'm pregnant with the Son of God? It was hard enough for me to believe, and I at least had an angel telling me. I keep rehearsing what to say, but nothing sounds quite right – 'Joseph, I've got some news . . .' 'Joseph, do you like children?' Joseph is such a good man, so respected in our community. We're not even married yet – what will this do to his reputation? Oh, it's no good. However I phrase this, it all comes down to the same thing. I just have to tell him. 'Joseph, I'm pregnant.'

Going from a spiritual high, a 'mountain top' experience, back down to earth with a bump when the rest of the world kicks in.
Nearly all Christians will have experienced this in one way or another.

Let's look at Elijah, 1 Kings 18,19:

Elijah has just had a wonderful triumph over the worshippers of the pagan god, Baal. On Mount Carmel, Elijah showed them who the true God really is.
God sent fire from heaven!
Everyone acknowledged God as the true God, and he'd used Elijah to show them. And then all the prophets of Baal were killed.

Elijah must have been buzzing,
feeling so close to God,
on a real spiritual high . . .

But what do we read in the next chapter?

Elijah is on the run.
Queen Jezebel was not happy that he killed the prophets of Baal and she wants revenge.

Elijah is terrified and running for his life.
You could say, he's back down to earth with a bump.

Eventually, exhausted, he sits down and prays that he will die.

And God's reply to this prayer? 'Get up and eat.'

Clearly, God does not consider this to be the time for Elijah's death.
Eating would not be necessary if Elijah was about to die.

It can be easy to lose perspective when things seem stacked against you.

Remember, God has a plan for your life.
He can always get you back on track,
just as he did for Elijah.

Having something to eat ensured that Elijah took time out.

We read, in 1 Kings 19, that Elijah ate and drank, then, strengthened by the food, he travelled on.

God knew what Elijah needed better than Elijah did.

Elijah thought he needed to die when God knew that he just needed a break.

It's OK to take time out.

Sometimes, we *need* to take time out.

We need to give ourselves a break.

We need to let God renew us.

We need to listen when he tells us to
'Be still, and know that I am God' (Psalm 46:10).

And we need to do it.

Lord God,

It's easy for me to think I know what I need.
Sometimes I find it difficult to wait to hear you tell me what I really do need.
Maybe that's because I'm always on the go.
Help me to take a break with you before I reach breaking point.

Amen

Mary's memo

Take time out
with God

My response:

Day 10

OK, so I told him. I just came out and said it. 'I'm pregnant.' I don't know how I expected him to react. Maybe shout? Hit something? (Hopefully) say everything would be OK? But any of those things would have been better than what happened. The colour drained from his face. I've heard that expression before but have never really seen it, not until now. He went grey and I thought he was going to collapse or something. When he did speak, it was in a calm, controlled voice: 'We'll talk about this tomorrow.' Then he was gone. And I was left standing there all alone. I am dreading tomorrow . . .

Have you ever dreaded tomorrow?
Maybe because of an exam, a hospital appointment, an interview . . .?

Let's look at Hannah, 1 Samuel 1:

Hannah was blessed in many ways.
She had a husband who loved her,
who provided for her,
who was a real man of God.

And yet, Hannah dreaded tomorrow.

Why?

Because Hannah longed to have a child.

And every 'tomorrow' brought another day of being reminded that she was childless.

Another day of being reminded by her husband's other wife that *she* had lots of children.

So what did Hannah do?

She prayed.

She told God.

'This is hard.
I'm miserable.
I'm bitter.
I'm dreading tomorrow.'

In other words, 'Help me.'

'I have been praying here out of my great anguish and grief' (v. 16).

Now, we know that Hannah did indeed become pregnant, but she wasn't to know that. Not at the time.

But still she prayed.
She kept the lines of communication between her and
God open.
Even in the midst of her distress, her bitterness, her misery,
she told him exactly how she was feeling.

And that was OK!

Hannah gave it to God, and God dealt with it.

Be honest with God.

Let him in and let him deal with it.

Psalm 86:7 (NLT):
*'I will call to you whenever I'm in trouble, and you
will answer me.'*

'Do not be afraid of tomorrow – God is already there'
(Unknown).

Lord God,

Right now, I am feeling . . .
I give these feelings to you.
I want to be like Hannah, to keep lines of
communication between you and me open.
Please help.

Amen

Mary's memo

Give it to God

My response:

Day 11

Well, tomorrow is here and it's a good job I gave it to God. I couldn't take this on my own . . . Joseph came round this morning and said he wants to separate. I am devastated. Marrying him is all I want to do. He said he will try to keep it as quiet as possible, away from the gossips. See, that's why I like him, he's so considerate – he knows that everyone would blame me for this pregnancy and he still wants to protect me. But the bottom line is that he wants to split up. He said he's just trying to do the right thing.

Knowing the right thing to do is not always easy . . .

Let's look at Daniel, in the book of Daniel:

Daniel constantly tried to do the right thing, the godly thing, in a culture that was increasingly ungodly.

He managed to stand firm about what food he ate, refusing to eat food that, according to God's law, was defiled.

He stood firm when required to interpret a dream for the king, giving a true interpretation regardless of the fact that the king probably wouldn't like it.

He saw his friends stand firm, even though refusing to worship an image of gold meant they would be thrown into a fiery furnace.

You could say that Daniel knew about standing firm, about doing the right thing.

And then comes another test – don't pray to anyone except the king for the next thirty days.

Here is a problem.

Daniel always prayed to God three times a day,
by his open window.
Anyone could see him.
So, what to do?

Maybe it would be OK to shut the window when he was praying, or pray in a different room . . . he wouldn't stop praying to God, just try to hide it a bit.

But, no! Daniel put God first.

He didn't change his routine.

He didn't worry about what people thought.

He did the right thing . . . and just carried on, regardless.

Which got him thrown into a den of lions.

Which allowed him to see God work mightily by shutting the lions' mouths so they didn't hurt Daniel.

Which led to the king turning to the living God.

Which led to the king telling everyone in the land about the living God.

And all because Daniel did the right thing and stuck with God.

Psalm 84:10 (NLT):
'A single day in your courts is better than a thousand anywhere else!'

If Daniel hadn't done the right thing, if he hadn't listened to God, he'd have missed out on seeing God work in amazing ways.

If we don't do the right thing, if we don't follow where God leads, we will miss out on seeing just how mighty God is.

Lord God,

Please help me to listen to you.
To listen, so that I can do the right thing . . .
So that I can do whatever you want me to do,
even when it's hard.
I don't want to miss out!

Amen

Mary's memo

Do the right thing

My response:

Day 12

Well, here's a change – my last diary entry seems like a distant nightmare. Everything is sorted now. Joseph had a visit from an angel, too, only his was in a dream. And the angel basically told him the same thing he'd told me. I have to say, Joseph isn't one for hanging around once he's made up his mind. As soon as he woke up, he came round to our house and said he was taking me home with him. Now I'm his wife! When we got home, I asked him what had changed his mind. 'Apart from being given a vision by God, you mean?' (He thinks his jokes are really funny.) Then he told me that it was actually four little words from God – 'Do not be afraid.'

Let's look at Joshua.

Joshua was Moses' assistant.

He led the troops in battle at Moses' command . . .

He went up the mountain with Moses and witnessed the awesome presence of God . . .

He saw Moses' righteous anger at the Israelites when

they worshipped a golden calf . . .
And suddenly, Moses, Joshua's mentor, leader and friend, is dead.

Not only dead, but leaving a daunting legacy.

The book of Deuteronomy concludes with these words;

'No-one has ever shown the mighty power or performed the awesome deeds that Moses did in the sight of all Israel' (34:12).

Moses must have been an amazing man.

Then, turn the page to Joshua chapter 1, and God is commanding Joshua to take over!

Take over from Moses?

Be Moses' assistant, OK.
Work with Moses, OK.
Learn from Moses, OK.

But *take over* from Moses?

Now that's different.

And what does God say to Joshua?

'Do not be afraid.'
And when God says, 'Do not be afraid,' he means it.

There's no need to be afraid when God is with you.

So Joshua steps up to the plate and tells the people,

'Get ready, we're going. I'm going God's way . . . I'm not afraid.'

Psalm 56:3,4 (NLT):
'When I am afraid, I will put my trust in you . . .
why should I be afraid?'

Lord God,

Sometimes life is hard.
I get worried.
I get scared.
Help me to say with the psalmist,
'When I am afraid, I will trust in you.'
And please help me to do it.

Amen

Mary's memo

Don't be afraid

My response:

Day 13

My life is a roller coaster at the moment . . . up, down, up, down. Yesterday was definitely an up, today is a down. I thought people would at least try to be happy for me, but no. It's not only that they aren't happy, they're definitely _not_ happy. People walk by me on the road as if they haven't seen me, though I know they have. They break into huddles round the cooking pots and don't let me in. If they do speak to me, it's just to be rude and call me crazy. I know it's because I'm pregnant, but when I try to explain, they don't want to know. Joseph found me in the house crying earlier and what he said brought me such comfort. He told me that not only did the angel tell him not to be afraid, he told him what the baby will be called. In fact, he'll have lots of names. One name will be Jesus, one name will be Immanuel . . . I looked at Joseph, wide-eyed. 'Yes,' he said. 'Immanuel, meaning, God with us.' I look down and smile. He's with me.

Have you ever been ostracized, ignored, bullied for your faith?

Let's look at David, 1 Samuel 17:

The Israelite army is fed up. Morale is low. They just haven't got anyone who can possibly fight against Goliath: the giant of a man their enemies, the Philistines, keep parading before them. Every day, Goliath taunts the Israelites and, every day, their confidence sinks a little lower.

Enter David.

David is a shepherd, not a soldier.
He's only at the battleground because he's come to see his soldier brothers.

When he finds them, they all start chatting and, in the middle of the conversation, David hears a shout.

Someone is shouting, threatening, defying the Israelites to find just one man to fight Goliath.

David looks around.

His brothers look scared.

In fact, everyone looks scared.

Then David becomes indignant.

How dare anyone threaten the Israelites like that! Don't they know that God is for Israel? That he's promised to never leave them or forsake them?

Just as the giant turns away, a voice rings out. It's David.
'I'll go!'

Everyone looks at the shepherd boy in stunned
silence.

Eventually, the Israelite king, Saul, offers David the use
of his armour, his tunic and his sword to fight Goliath.

David refuses.

In the end, all David takes with him are his sling and a
few stones –
the tools that God has helped him use successfully in his
life as a shepherd.

Of course, when Goliath sees David coming, he thinks
he's already won.

He mocks David,
ridicules David,
taunts David . . .
and is killed by David.

Killed by David who, to outward appearances, didn't
stand a chance.

Killed by David who had God with him, and so Goliath
never stood a chance.

Psalm 139:8

*'If I go up to the heavens, you are there; if I make
my bed in the depths, you are there.'*

Lord God,

Thank you that you are with me,
wherever I go,
however people treat me,
whatever they say to me.
Please help me to remember that.
Help me to know that you are my Immanuel.

Amen

Mary's memo

God is with me

My response:

Day 14

I've decided to go and visit Elizabeth. I hope she'll be
pleased to see me. I'm nervous, though; she might treat
me as everyone else has been. She's my cousin, but
probably because she's so much older than me, we've
never really had much in common until now. Who
would have thought we'd be pregnant at the same time?
I'm really pleased for Elizabeth; she's wanted a child for
so long. Hopefully she'll be pleased for me, too. I haven't
seen her for ages. We don't stay in touch as much as we
should but we are family, after all. And our babies have
brought us together. Well, I guess it's my baby really.
If it wasn't for the angel coming to me and telling me
I am pregnant, he wouldn't have told me that Elizabeth
is pregnant, and I wouldn't be going to visit her . . .
yes, it is Jesus that's brought us together.

How do you get on with other people?
In your family?
At school or work?
Your friends?
People at church?

It can be hard to get along with other people all the
time, can't it?

Sometimes people just unintentionally drift apart, but sometimes we disagree and fall out.

When this happens, we need to let Jesus bring us together.
Let him heal relationships, hurts, bitterness . . .

Let's look at 1 Corinthians 13:

'Love is patient.'
Love is, but sometimes we're not.

What does the Bible say?
1 Thessalonians 5:14: 'be patient with everyone.'
2 Peter 3:9: 'The Lord . . . is patient with you'.

'Love is kind.'
Love is, but sometimes we're not.

What does the Bible say?
Ephesians 4:32: 'Be kind and compassionate to one another'.
James 5:11: 'The Lord is full of compassion'.

'Love is not proud.'
Love isn't, but sometimes we are.

What does the Bible say?
Romans 12:16: 'Do not be proud'.
Psalm 147:6: 'The LORD sustains the humble'.

'Love keeps no record of wrongs.'
Love doesn't, but sometimes we do.

What does the Bible say?
Colossians 3:13: 'Forgive as the Lord forgave you.'

Jesus commands us to 'Love each other as I have loved you (John 15:12).

How has Jesus loved you?

He put you before everything else – he gave up heaven to come to earth for you.

How have you loved other people?

By putting them first?
By loving them with Jesus' love?

How *will* you love other people this week, this month, this year?
With Jesus' love?

Think about how you can show Jesus' love to others.

Try it today . . .

Lord God,

Thank you that Jesus loves me so much that he gave up everything for me.
Lord, that is amazing.
I can't understand it but I know it's true.
Please help me to show Jesus' love to other people.
Help me to put them before myself.

Amen

Mary's memo

Love like Jesus

My response:

Day 15

I'm writing this from Elizabeth's house. I arrived safely and she was really pleased to see me. What a relief. And an amazing thing happened when I arrived. I had just seen Elizabeth and called 'hello' when she suddenly put her hands on her rounded stomach and bent over double. I was so scared. What if something had happened to her baby? So I hurried over, full of concern, but when I got to her I saw that she was laughing! She couldn't speak for laughing, just kept stroking her stomach, and her face was alight with joy. I was really unsure what to do so I just kind of hovered next to her. In the end, she managed to tell me what she was so happy about. Apparently, as soon as I'd called hello, her baby leaped in her womb. She said he was leaping for joy. I don't think I need have worried about being welcome . . .

Elizabeth's baby leaped in her womb when Mary, pregnant with Jesus, approached.

In other words, the baby got excited because Jesus was coming!

Let's look at Zacchaeus, Luke 19:1–10:

Day 15

Zacchaeus is a tax collector.
Nobody likes him.
He has lots of money, but no friends.

One day, Zacchaeus notices there is a buzz in the air.
People seem to be excited about something.
He looks around, but sees nothing unusual,
except that more people than is normal seem to be out
and about . . .

Not far away, he sees a group of people all talking at
once, their faces alight with anticipation. So he sneaks
up to them, hoping they won't notice, and tries to
listen. It's hard to make out what they're saying, but one
phrase is repeated again and again: 'Jesus is coming!'

And suddenly Zacchaeus realizes that he would actually
quite like to see this man, Jesus.
Just see him, mind.
Zacchaeus doesn't dare let himself think that Jesus
might be interested in him.
No one ever is.
But he wants to see Jesus anyway.

He climbs a tree to wait for Jesus, and hopefully get
a better view . . . and then nearly falls off his branch,
because Jesus stops right by his tree.

Zacchaeus can't believe it when Jesus speaks to him:
'Zacchaeus, I'm coming to your house today.'

What? No one ever wants to come and visit him.

Zacchaeus scrambles down from the tree.
Jesus is coming to his house!
Zacchaeus had two 'comings' that day:

He knew Jesus was coming, but had to wait.

When he went home, Jesus was coming with him.

You know, you can be like Zacchaeus.

You can be confident that Jesus is coming with you.

Whatever lies ahead of you, whatever the future holds,
Jesus is coming.
He'll be there.
You may have to wait for his timing, but he will be there.

Wherever you go,
whatever you do,
whatever you go through . . .
Jesus is coming with you.

You are not alone.

Matthew 28:20 (NLT):
*Jesus said, 'Be sure of this: I am with you always,
even to the end of the age.'*

Lord God,

Thank you that the story of Zacchaeus is in the Bible.
Thank you for the lesson that whatever happens, you are coming with me.
Thank you that you never leave me.

Amen

Mary's memo

Jesus is coming

My response:

Day 16

Wow. As if the 'baby leaping' thing wasn't enough, there was more to come . . . Elizabeth was filled with the Holy Spirit! She suddenly started speaking in a really loud voice. People were stopping to look at her. She was talking about how special my baby is and how wonderful it was to see us, how she felt humbled that we'd come but was so pleased that we had. She kept calling me blessed. I've never thought of it like that, but you know what? I am blessed. I really am. God is using me as he wants to – I don't think it's possible to be more blessed than that!

Elizabeth was in tune with God.

We don't read that she even knew Mary was pregnant before Mary arrived, let alone knew how special the baby was. And yet, here she is, rejoicing that the mother of her Lord has visited her.

How did Elizabeth know that Mary was pregnant?

Because she was in tune with God.

His timing.
His agenda.

Let's look at Philip, Acts 8:26–40:

One day, an angel told Philip to go and walk along a road.
A desert road, to be precise.
No explanation, he's just told to go.
So he goes.

As he's walking along, he sees an Ethiopian, an important official, riding along in a chariot and reading the book of Isaiah.

God's Spirit tells Philip,
'Go to the chariot and stay near it.'
No explanation, he's just told to go.
So he goes.

And because he listens to the Spirit, because he goes, he's able to take the opportunity to talk to the Ethiopian, share the good news of Jesus with him and even baptize him.

All because he was in tune with God.

And as soon as Philip has baptized the man, the Spirit of God takes him away again. And he ends up somewhere else, and shares the good news somewhere else . . .

All because Philip stayed in tune with God.
All because he wanted to be as close to God's will as he could be.

And so the good news spread.

Elizabeth was in tune with the Spirit.
Philip was in tune with the Spirit.
Mary was in tune with the Spirit.

Are you in tune with the Spirit?

Do you want to obey God more than anything?

Psalm 25:4:
'Show me your ways, O Lᴏʀᴅ, teach me your paths'.

One definition of 'blessed' is 'granted God's favour'.

Was Mary blessed? Yes!

The same God who granted favour and blessing to Mary, favours and blesses you.

Are you blessed? Yes!

Lord God,

I want to be like Philip.
And Elizabeth and Mary.
Thank you for their deep relationship with you.
Please help me to recognize how blessed I am.
Help me to hear your voice leading me, and help
me to obey.

Amen

Mary's memo

Stay in tune
with God

My response:

Day 17

Can't stop thinking about how good God is. I want to do more than just think about it; I feel as though I will burst! If I were clever, I'd write it all down. If I were an orator, I would make an impassioned speech. But I'm neither of those things. If I were a musician, I'd compose a beautiful piece of music . . . hang on, I can't play an instrument, but I can sing!

Do you ever find yourself thinking like this?
Focusing on what you can't do, rather than on what you can?

Let's see what we can learn from Mary's song, Luke 1:46–55:

Mary 'glorifies the Lord'.
That's the first thing she does.
She focuses on God before anything else.
Always the best thing to do, whatever your circumstances.

Mary is realistic about herself before God, calling herself 'humble' and a 'servant', not bigging herself up.

It can be easy to think, 'I *deserve* such and such.'
Now stop and consider who you are before God, from
Ephesians 2:

Dead in your transgressions and sins . . . and God made
you alive with Christ . . . nothing to do with anything
you've done, it is purely a gift from God.

Think about it . . . and now try to think about what you
think you deserve.

Puts things into perspective, doesn't it?

Mary is accepting:
'the Mighty One has done great things for me . . .'

In other words, if God is in this, it must be good!

Mary's situation may not have been one she'd have
chosen, at least not at first.
But as she sees God in it, her priorities, her desires
become the same as his.
She wants what God wants, regardless.

What about you?
Do you want what God wants, regardless?

Then Mary moves back to glorifying the Lord.

What a great example, to start and finish by glorifying God.

First, she glorifies him for who he is, then, having brought her will in line with his, she glorifies him for what he's done – she looks back at his faithfulness over the years.

She reminds herself that he is the same God now as he was then . . . *a God to count on*.

In his letter to the Colossian church, the apostle Paul tells the Christians that 'your life is now hidden with Christ in God' (Colossians 3:3).

Paul wanted people to look at the Colossian Christians and see God.

What a great thing to aim for!

What they couldn't do didn't matter.
What did matter was that God worked through them.

What do you want people to see when they look at you?

Do you want them to see God at work?

Day 17

Lord God,

Thank you for Mary's example.
Please help me to stop focusing on what I can't do, but on what I can.
What I can do because I belong to you.
What I can do to show you to others, because you are at work in me.

Amen

Mary's memo

Glorify God

My response:

Day 18

It's hard to believe I've been here for three months; the time has just flown by. It has been lovely spending time with Elizabeth. I don't think I've ever talked so much in my life – we've talked about anything and everything but, of course, mainly about our babies. It was exciting to put my hand on Elizabeth's tummy and feel her baby kicking. Soon, my baby will be kicking! I know I have to go home but I really don't want to. While I've been here, I've been able to forget everything, but now I have to go back and face the taunts, the sly looks, the whispering . . .

Have you ever been in this situation?
Scared to go back, afraid to face up to things?

What about with God?
Have you ever thought that things were so terrible that even God wouldn't want you?

Let's look at a parable Jesus told, in Luke 15:11–32:

A man has two sons.
Everything is fine; they all work together on his estate.

And then, one day, the younger son announces that he's leaving.

So the younger son leaves, becoming a smaller and smaller speck on the horizon until, at last, he disappears from sight.
But his father still watches for him.

The younger son, in a place far away, is having a great time, making new friends, going to parties.
He doesn't know it but, back at home, his father still watches for him.

Then the son finds things get a bit tricky – as his money runs out, so do his friends. He finds himself alone, wondering what to do.
He doesn't know it, but his father still watches for him.

Eventually, the son manages to get a job. Not a good job, but better than nothing. As he goes about his job, feeling more and more disheartened,
he doesn't know it, but his father still watches for him.

Finally, he's had enough. He resigns from his job and decides to set off for home. Maybe his father will give him some work; anything would be better than how things are at the moment. As he begins the long walk home,
he doesn't know it, but his father still watches for him.

He trudges on. His feet are sore, he's hot, he's thirsty, he's tired and bedraggled.
He doesn't know it, but his father still watches for him.

At last he can see the house in the distance.
His pace quickens but his eyes are downcast.
What on earth is he going to say to his father?
After all, his father had loved and cared for him for years, and what thanks did he get? His son just walked out without a backward glance.
Will his father ever forgive him?

He's sure his father won't want him as a son, but what if he doesn't even want him as a servant?
What if he won't even speak to him?
What if . . .
And suddenly, the son finds himself enveloped in a big bear hug.
It's his father.
'I love you, son. Welcome home.'

As they carry on down the road together, the son begins to apologize, over and over again.
Eventually, his father stops him:
'Son, I know.'
'But how can you know? Why would you be glad to see me if you know? Why would you love me if you know? I was miles away. I forgot about you, didn't give you a second thought.'

His father stops, puts his hands on his son's shoulders and, looking deep into his eyes, says,

'I know because I never stopped watching for you.'

Whatever you've done, whatever you've said or thought, whatever bits of you you've tried to hide, why not return to God?
He knows about them anyway. He's always watching for you.

Return completely to him.

Won't it be great to hear him say,
'I love you. Welcome home.'

Zephaniah 3:17 (NLT):

'The LORD . . . will take delight in you . . . He will rejoice over you with joyful songs.'

Lord God,

Thank you that no matter what I've done,
you are always watching for me.
You always want me back.
Help me not to leave it too long . . .

Amen

Mary's memo

God's watching for me

My response:

Day 19

Well, I've been home for a few months now, and gradually things have got better. When I first arrived home from Elizabeth's, some of the things people said to me were pretty awful, but I just kept reminding myself that God is with me and that I've done nothing wrong. I went to the market this morning, and for the first time in ages, people hardly paid me any attention as I walked along. Not even a second glance or a whispered remark – it was bliss!

When I got home, Joseph was there, which is unusual for him at that time of day. I should have known things were becoming too good to be true – apparently, we all have to go to Bethlehem. At least, all the people, like Joseph and me, who are descended from David. I've only just got settled back in Nazareth, and now I have to go somewhere new? Start again? Start again with the taunts, comments, whispers . . .? And this time, I am _really_ pregnant. I mean, the baby could come any time now. How am I supposed to travel? Oh, I don't want to go to Bethlehem!

Do you know what it feels like to have to go where you don't want to go?

Perhaps God is leading you in a new direction and you want to say, 'No, stop! I'm happy where I am.'

Let's look at another Joseph, Genesis 37,39–50:

Joseph is 17.
He is good-looking.
He is a shepherd.
He has eleven brothers.
He is his father's favourite.

Life is good – but his brothers don't think so.

They are jealous of Joseph. They can't understand why he is the favourite.
And then, to cap it all, Joseph has some prophetic dreams, which basically say that all the brothers will bow down before Joseph!

This is just too much.
The brothers decide to sell Joseph as a slave, and he ends up in Egypt.

He *really* doesn't want to go.
Why would he?
Life is pretty good as it is.

In Egypt, Joseph is brought to the attention of Potiphar, one of Pharaoh's top officials, and becomes chief of his household.

Life is good again, but Potiphar's wife doesn't think so. She wants Joseph for herself.

It becomes an obsession with her and, when Joseph refuses to sleep with her, she traps him and has him thrown into jail.

Joseph *really* doesn't want to go.
Why would he?
Life (apart from Potiphar's wife) is pretty good as it is.

While in prison, Joseph quickly rises through the ranks and is given charge over the prisoners. One day, Joseph interprets some dreams, one of which gets a man out of prison and back serving Pharaoh. The man promises to remember Joseph and put in a kind word for him . . . but he doesn't.
And Joseph is still stuck in prison.

He *really* doesn't want to stay there.
Why would he?
Life is pretty grim in jail.

But a few years later, the man remembers Joseph.
Pharaoh needs a dream interpreting and the ex-prisoner knows just the man to do it.

And (to cut a long story short) Joseph solves the dream, saves the nation from famine and is reconciled with his family.

The nation was saved because Joseph went, again and again, where he really didn't want to go.

What might God have in store for you?

1 Corinthians 2:9 (NLT):
'No eye has seen, no ear has heard, and no mind has imagined what God has prepared for those who love him.'

Lord God,

Thank you that this verse from 1 Corinthians is true.
I can't even begin to imagine the things you have in store for me!
Help me to remember that you see the bigger picture.
Help me to trust you when you move me on.

Amen

Mary's memo

Go with God

My response:

Day 20

Am currently en route to Bethlehem. As expected, this journey is not easy. Joseph is walking and I am on the donkey. Have you ever tried to keep your balance on a donkey while 9 months pregnant?! It is hard and I'm so tired. I just can't get comfortable – what I really need is some shade, but that's impossible. The sun is beating down and there is nowhere to shelter on the road. I know this sounds really moany and complaining but I am so fed up. The journey seems to be taking forever. I just have to keep focusing on the fact that we're being obedient by going to Bethlehem. We're doing what's right.

Sometimes it's hard to be obedient, isn't it?

Let's look at Ananias, Acts 9:

Ananias was a man who followed God.

One day, he had a vision in which the Lord told him to go and see a man named Saul, in Damascus.

Sounds fairly straightforward so far . . . but Ananias knew about Saul.

He knew that Saul had basically made it his life's mission to persecute Christians.

Ananias knew why Saul had come to Damascus – to arrest all the people there who followed Jesus.

Which would include Ananias.

As if that wasn't bad enough, there was more . . . the Lord told Ananias not only to go and see Saul, but to go right up close to him and put his hands over Saul's blinded eyes, to restore his sight.

Things were becoming more difficult for Ananias by the minute!

But God told him to go and do the right thing, regardless.

And the right thing was to do something he didn't want to do.

God had given Ananias a job to do and he knew that Ananias could be relied upon.

So, Ananias went, in fear and trepidation . . . and God used him to kick-start the ministry of Saul, the Apostle to the Gentiles.

Saul (who became Paul) nurtured, taught, preached to, loved, cared for and encouraged a vast proportion of the early church – and it started when Ananias put himself, his desires, his feelings to one side and was obedient.

Can God rely on you to do the right thing for him, to obey him, even when it's tough?

Psalm 18:30:
'As for God, his way is perfect.'

Lord God,

Your way is perfect, I know that.
Please help me to always make the decision to follow your way for me,
even when I don't really want to.

Amen

Mary's memo

Obey God's way

My response:

Day 21

Finally, we've reached Bethlehem. I think I could sleep for a week! The only problem is, everyone else seems to have arrived in Bethlehem, too – the place is packed. The hotels and inns are all overflowing and quite a few have turned us away. As I said to Joseph, maybe we should just find a spot under a tree or something. I can't believe that there is literally no room in any of the hotels. It's strange how, surrounded by lots of noise and bustle, but with nowhere to go and no one to turn to, unwanted by everybody, I feel lonelier than I've ever felt in my life . . .

Have you ever felt lonely? Unwanted?
Despite all of life going on around you?

Let's look at a woman who felt just like that, in Luke 8:40–48:

Jesus is walking along, surrounded by crowds of people. He's very popular and, of course, everyone wants to talk to him, to walk with him, to see him.

Now, imagine you are a woman who has been bleeding for twelve years.

You've heard that Jesus can heal people, and you desperately want him to heal you. You've heard on the grapevine which way he will be heading.

You'd do anything to see Jesus . . . but you are bleeding.

And that makes you unclean, an outcast.
Someone who nobody wants to speak to,
let alone come into contact with.

So, you have a dilemma – face rejection from people or miss out on seeing Jesus.
Miss out on the possibility of being healed.

The main problem is that crowds follow him wherever he goes.
You've spent twelve years avoiding people and being avoided by them, but now, if you're going to take this chance, you have to go in amongst the crowd.

You set off after Jesus a number of times, but always lose courage and turn back. You see groups of friends following Jesus, chatting as they go.
But you don't have friends.
People don't want to chat with you.
People don't even notice you.

You feel lonely and dejected as once more you turn for home.

Then, one day, somehow you find a bit of extra courage.
You don't turn back as you near the crowd.
Instead, you quietly weave through the throng, moving
closer to Jesus.

Eventually, you find yourself right behind him.
You open your mouth to speak . . . but no words come.
The old fear is back –
Will Jesus reject you?
What about all the people?
When they notice you, it will be obvious that you are on
your own,
that you have no one to talk to,
that you are unclean.

You feel crushed and deflated and, instinctively, your
hand reaches out towards Jesus. And touches his cloak.
And your bleeding stops.
It actually stops. Just like that.

You turn and try to sneak, unseen, back through the
crowd, but the crowd has stopped moving.
In fact, it stopped so suddenly that all the people are
bumping into each other.

And that's when you hear the voice: 'Who touched me?'

You try to shrink into the ground, hoping the crowd
will start moving, but then you hear the voice again,
'Someone has touched me.'

Your heart thuds painfully, but you know you have to turn around . . . and, when you do, Jesus is there.

You fall at his feet.
Then you tell all the people, the people who wouldn't talk to you or listen to you before, that you have been healed. And Jesus says to you,
'Daughter, go in peace.'

At the start of this passage in Luke, she is an unnamed woman.
At the end, a beloved daughter of Jesus.
Accepted, wanted, never to be lonely again –
part of his family.

2 Corinthians 5:17 (NLT):
'Anyone who belongs to Christ has become a new person.
The old life is gone; a new life has begun!'

Lord God,

Thank you that I am never unwanted, even if I feel it.
Because you always want me.
Thank you for bringing me into your family.
Thank you for making me new.

Amen

Mary's memo

I am a new creation

My response:

Day 22

As I said, it is so crowded here. Wherever we go, people are pushing and shoving. Everyone is desperate to find somewhere to sleep. We can't find anywhere! As we were looking for a place to stay, I felt a sharp pain. And another. 'Joseph,' I called, but he didn't hear me over the general hubbub. I tried again, this time louder: 'Joseph!' He turned round, eyes full of concern. 'Joseph, the baby is coming!' Concern turned to speechless panic. I wanted to shake him – 'What are we going to do? Joseph, it's time!'

What 'time' is it in your life?
Time for God to work?

Let's look at Matthew 14:22–33:

Jesus has sent his disciples ahead of him in their boat, to row to the other side of the lake. They are experienced fishermen; rowing a boat is second nature to them.

They are rowing along when suddenly the boat begins to tip over a bit . . . then a bit more . . . then a bit more . . . and they realize that they are in the middle of a full-blown storm.

And they are terrified.
(It must have been some storm to scare fishermen witless!)

Then, as if they aren't scared enough, they see a ghost walking on the water.

By now they are almost out of their minds with fear . . . until the ghost speaks.
And it's not a ghost, it is Jesus.

The disciples heave sighs of relief – except for Peter.
He has no time for that; he wants proof that it really is Jesus.

So he says, 'Jesus, if it's really you, tell me to come to you on the water.'
And Jesus replies, 'Come!'

Now Peter has a choice.
Stay in the relative safety of the boat without Jesus, or step out of the boat onto the stormy water with Jesus.

And Peter chooses the latter.
He chooses to be with Jesus.
He chooses to step out of the boat.

And he walks on water.

Yet, as he walks, he stops looking at Jesus.
He notices again the storm crashing round him, he
begins to sink . . .
and Jesus lifts him up.

And helps him walk again.

And Peter returns to the boat,
walking on the water
with Jesus.

It's doubtful that Peter ever regretted getting out of that
boat to be with Jesus.

Even though he did begin to sink,
even though he took his eye off Jesus,
even though he didn't do it all right . . .
he didn't regret it, because Jesus was with him.

Jesus was stretching Peter's faith.
It was time for Peter to do something new.
And he walked on water.

Maybe the only people with regrets that day were the
disciples who stayed in the boat,
stayed with what they knew,
and missed out on walking on water with Jesus.

What time is it in your life?
Is God challenging you?

Telling you that it's time to move on in your relationship with him?
Time to step out of your comfort zone?

If so, don't live with regrets and 'what ifs'.

Keep your eyes on Jesus, and you can do anything he's asking of you.

Fix your eyes on Jesus and step out of the boat.

As Hebrews 12:2 (NLT) says, keep '[y]our eyes on Jesus, the champion who initiates and perfects [y]our faith.'

> *Lord God,*
>
> *Thank you that when you encourage me to get out of the boat,*
> *you are there beside me.*
> *You meet me.*
> *Sometimes I feel as though I am drowning –*
> *help me to keep looking at you instead of thrashing about on my own.*
>
> *Amen*

Mary's memo

It's time

My response:

Day 23

Panic, panic, panic! Joseph is dashing from door to door, begging people to let us in. I am closing my eyes and trying to pretend that this is not happening to me. We are barely stopping ourselves from becoming hysterical. The baby is coming! We've been turned away countless times now. Joseph is knocking on another door. I am surprised that we are not turned away immediately but, after some conversation, are led inside . . . and through the house . . . past the sleeping area . . . What's going on? Then I see the stable, smelly and full of animals. Joseph is pointing to it and nodding. Suddenly I realize. You've got to be joking, I can't give birth there!

In the light of what Mary had already been through, maybe giving birth in a stable was not high on the list of difficulties.
Maybe it was a 'small' thing to do, but she still had to do it.

Let's look at John 6:1–15:

Jesus wants some time alone, but he's not going to get it. As soon as the crowds of people hear where he is, they follow him, they go where he is going, they do whatever

they can to be with Jesus.
And Jesus welcomes them.
He teaches them, heals them, cares for them. And they
hang onto his every word. Time passes, unnoticed.

Eventually, when it begins to get dark, some of Jesus'
disciples come up to have a quiet word with him:
'Jesus, perhaps we should send these people home now.
It's late, and they'll need some food' (see Mark 6:35,36).

The disciples clearly think that Jesus is going to agree
with them, to do what they say, to fit in with their timing
– but they have another think coming . . .

Jesus replies that not only do the people need to stay,
but that the disciples are in charge of making sure they
get some food. What?!
Eight months' salary wouldn't buy enough food for this
crowd!
They look at each other, totally stumped.

Then Andrew notices a small boy, standing nearby with
a packed lunch.
The silence is becoming awkward now, and none of
the others is saying anything, so Andrew doubtfully
mentions the boy to Jesus,
'This boy has five loaves and two fish. But that's not
enough for a crowd this size.'

But in Jesus' hands, it is.

It is more than enough.
And the entire crowd is fed.

The disciples thought they were sorted with Jesus.
They knew where they stood and what he wanted from them.
So far in the gospels, we read that he wanted them to go where he went and to do what he told them, which had worked fine – until now.

Now Jesus wanted to move them on, to challenge them, to make their faith grow.

Is it time for your faith to grow?

Maybe, in this story, the boy got much more than he gave to Jesus.
Imagine the wonder he would have felt as he offered his lunch and it fed a crowd.
The boy did a 'little' thing, and Jesus turned it into something big for his own glory.

However small the things we do or give for Jesus may seem to us,
he turns them into something big for his glory.

Mary said 'yes' to God.

Yes in the big things (giving birth to Jesus), but also yes in the small things (giving birth in a stable).

Sometimes it can be easy to think that the small things we do don't matter.

But they do.

They matter to God.

And with God, there are no 'little' things, anyway. Everything we do for him is important, is vital, is big.

Matthew 25:21:
'Well done, good and faithful servant! You have been faithful with a few things'.

Or, to put it another way, this servant had been faithful with small things.

Can the same be said of you?

Lord God,

Help me to be a faithful servant.
Please grow my faith by helping me to be faithful in small things . . .
I want to glorify you in any way I can.

Amen

Mary's memo

Little is big with God

My response:

Day 24

Jesus is born!
   Finally, I am watching my beautiful baby boy sleeping. He's perfect! He makes everything worth it:
   The shock that I was pregnant, Joseph potentially leaving me, the comments and taunts from the people in the village, the journey to Bethlehem, the feeling of having nowhere to go, having to give birth in a stable . . . it was all worth it. I've held my baby in my arms at last and nothing else matters – Jesus is born!

Paul said, in Philippians 3:8,10 (NLT):
'Everything . . . is worthless when compared with the infinite value of knowing Christ Jesus my Lord . . . I want to know Christ'.

Do you want to know Christ Jesus?

To know him and know him and know him
until nothing else matters
because you have Jesus?

Jesus wants you to.
He wants you to spend more time with him,
to get to know him,

to worship him,
to serve him,
to talk to him
to let him help you . . .

To remember that, whatever happens or has happened,
you'll be OK if you stick with him.

Jesus wants you to celebrate because he was born for you!

'A child is born to you,
A son is given to you;
And he will be called

Wonderful Counsellor,

Mighty God,

Everlasting Father,

Prince of Peace

(see Isaiah 9:6).

> *Lord God,*
>
> *Thank you for sending Jesus.*
> *And thank you that you did it for me.*
>
> *Amen*

Mary's memo

Jesus was born for me

My response:

Day 25

Well, I have not really had much time to keep my diary since Jesus was born, he keeps me so busy – it's been a couple of years now, and I can't remember ever not having him around. I love every minute of life with Jesus!

He's having a nap right now and I could not resist using the time to update my diary. I know I should probably do the washing or something but this is much more important . . .

Not long after Jesus was born, we had some visitors at the stable. I was pretty surprised that these people even ventured into town – they are not normally welcome and tend to stay out in the hills with their sheep. But these shepherds turned up – apparently some angels had told them to come to see Jesus. Well, I know all about being visited by an angel! To be honest, I was a bit unsure about them at first. But of course, I was more than happy to show off my son, and the shepherds were so excited to see him. They couldn't stop looking at Jesus, and they just kept thanking God for him, over and over again. When they eventually left, I could hear them singing and laughing as they walked along.

Then, just a few weeks ago, we had some more visitors arrive. These visitors were the total opposite of the shepherds. They were wise men, who had come all the way from the East on their camels. What an honour for us! They had come because a star had told them to. What I mean is, they studied the stars, saw a new one and followed it until it stopped over the house where we are now staying.

Of course, when they told me that, I went outside and looked up at the sky – and they were right, there was a bright star directly over the house.

The wise men had brought gifts for Jesus – gold, frankincense and myrrh – and they bowed down before Jesus when they gave them to him. I have to say that it looked a bit strange, these wise and learned men in their beautiful clothes, bowing down before my little boy.

In today's diary, Mary records two lots of visitors, both at opposite ends of the social scale.
The shepherds, poor and outcast. The wise men, rich and respected.
And yet, beyond initial appearances, beneath the surface, there are some similarities between these two groups.
Let's have a look:

Both the shepherds and the wise men were getting on with their jobs (looking after sheep/stargazing) when the good news about Jesus came to them.

They didn't have to go anywhere special.
They didn't have to say anything special.
The good news came to where they were.

Wherever you go, whatever you do, whatever you
become . . .
God's good news is there.
God is there.
He can reach you.
You just need to look up.

The shepherds looked up and saw the angels.
The wise men looked up and saw the star.
Two different things, but both put there by God.

And both things led them to Jesus.
Both gave them guidance. Both gave them direction.

Will you look up and see God pointing you in his
direction?
Telling you the way to find him, again and again?

Both the shepherds and the wise men came to Jesus
and, in their coming, they overcame.

The shepherds overcame a feeling of not being good
enough to come.

Their physical journey may not have been too hard; they
only had to travel from the outskirts of Bethlehem.

But the emotional journey they made was huge.
These men were social outcasts.
They knew they would not be welcome in town.

And so they had a decision to make –
Were they going to allow their fear of rejection to stop
them from coming to Jesus?

Are you?

The wise men overcame a feeling of being 'too good' to
bow before a 2-year-old boy.

Their physical journey was longer than that of the
shepherds. It was more difficult. Mile after mile on their
camels – but at least they had camels.
And wealth. And status.
And yet, when they saw Jesus, when they saw
the 2-year-old boy standing there, they humbled
themselves and bowed before him.

They realized that their wealth and success paled into
insignificance before Jesus. Before God.

The wise men made a wise decision – they gave Jesus
his proper place.

Do you?

Lord God,

Thank you that you are a God who accepts me, whenever I come to you.
I'm sorry for not accepting myself sometimes.
And for letting this lack of acceptance get in the way of my relationship with you.
Help me to remember to look up and see you pointing me in the right direction – in your direction.
And please help me to come.

Amen

Mary's memo

Come to Jesus

My response:

Day 26

Have found my diary again; I've only ignored it for about ten years! And I was doing so well with it, too, before Jesus was born. I haven't ignored it on purpose; it is just that life has been so busy. Jesus is doing really well. He is growing strong and healthy, clever, close to God – all the things I would want for my boy. He is 12 now, can you believe it? Which reminds me, that is why I have dug out my diary . . . like lots of families, we go to Jerusalem every year to celebrate the Feast of Passover. I can hardly believe what happened while we were there this time . . .

We walked to Jerusalem in a group, as usual, and when we got there, it was absolutely packed with people, as it always is at Passover. We had a week of remembering all that God has done for us, then we set off for home. There were crowds of people leaving Jerusalem, and we all walked along together.

At the end of the first day of travelling, I asked Joseph to tell Jesus to stay near us, since it was getting dark. 'He's not with me,' said Joseph, who had been deep in conversation with Matthew, our neighbour. 'I assumed you were keeping an eye on him.' I replied that I had assumed the same thing about Joseph. We looked at each other and realized the terrible truth – we had lost Jesus!

I think the last time I panicked so much was when I was in Bethlehem, ready to give birth to Jesus but with nowhere to go. There was nothing for it, we had to go back. So Joseph and I left the group heading away from Jerusalem and retraced our steps.

We made it to Jerusalem and started searching everywhere we could think of. We tried all the places that we'd been to during Passover. No Jesus. Then we tried the places we hadn't been to. No Jesus. After three days of this, we realized that we were beginning to go round in circles, trying places that we had already searched.

Then Joseph realized that we had not looked in the Temple. The words were hardly out of his mouth when I was off, and he had to hurry to catch me. We arrived, breathless, at the Temple, and what did we see? Jesus sitting there, talking with the teachers. And people were listening to him! In fact, they were amazed at how much he knew. So were Joseph and I, but after a minute I began to feel annoyed. Joseph and I had been out of our minds with worry and here was Jesus, sitting there as calm as you like!

I asked Jesus what he was thinking of. Why had he treated us in this way? Didn't he know that we would be worried and looking for him?

And all he wanted to know was why we had been looking for him? Apparently, we should have known that he'd be 'in his Father's house', as he put it!

Anyway, Jesus came back to Nazareth with us and has been good as gold ever since. No more disappearing acts . . .

So, Mary and Joseph lost Jesus (Luke 2:41–52).

Let's think about how that happened:

Mary and Joseph set off with Jesus.
They walked beside him.
Maybe chatted with him.
Then they took their eyes off him and started chatting to other people,
looking at other things, assuming Jesus was with them.
And, when they turned round, they could not find Jesus . . .

How about you?

Maybe you have set off with Jesus.
You have started a journey with him.
Chatted with him.
Shared your life with him.

And then you took your eyes off him.
Maybe just for a second. You thought you'd give church a miss one week, you skipped reading your Bible one week, you forgot to pray one week, you forgot to consult him about your plans . . . and one week turned

into two, and three, and you just carried on with your life.

Carried on with your life, assuming that Jesus was going along with you and your plans.
But when you did eventually turn round, you could not see Jesus.
You knew he must be there somewhere, but you just couldn't see him.

Maybe that's you right now.
You can't see Jesus.
Not as you used to see him, talk with him, walk with him.

Remember the verse from Psalm 139?
'If I go up to the heavens, you are there;
if I make my bed in the depths, you are there.'

Wherever you go, Jesus is there. But maybe, to find him, you'll need to do what Mary and Joseph did. You'll need to get away from the distractions and the noise, and get back to the place, physically or emotionally, where you can be with Jesus again.

When Mary and Joseph located Jesus, he was surprised that they had found it so hard to find him. Why?
Because they should have know where he would be.

They should have known.

It was Mary and Joseph that had moved away;
Jesus hadn't gone anywhere.

Have you moved away from Jesus?
Well, he hasn't gone anywhere.
He's waiting, but it is up to you.
You can find him if you want to.
Find him and keep finding him.
Every day, in every situation . . .

And, when you do find him, like the teachers in the
Temple who listened to Jesus – prepare to be amazed!

Lord God,

I am sorry that I take my eyes off you.
I don't mean to, but it happens.
And then it is hard to find you again.
Thank you that you don't go anywhere.
Help me to find you, and keep finding you, every
day.

Amen

Mary's memo

Find Jesus

My response:

Day 27

I love weddings! There has been one in the village this week and I went along. So did Jesus – hard to believe he is 30 now. I don't know where the time has gone; it's a good thing that this diary is patient! Anyway, we were having a great time. It was a brilliant party and everyone was having fun . . . but then the wine ran out. It is not safe to drink water here so, basically, there was nothing to drink. I felt so sorry for the hosts and wished I could do something to help, but I couldn't – all I could think to do was tell Jesus that the wine had run out. So I did. But he just asked me why I was telling him. He said his time had not yet come, whatever that meant. There was no chance to try and puzzle it out right then, so I just told the servants to do whatever Jesus told them to do. Honestly, it was not a good time to start speaking in riddles, so one of us had to be clear!

Jesus told the servants to fill some big jars with water and then pour the water for the master of the banquet to drink. I have to say, my mind hesitated at that – wouldn't it be better to try a drop ourselves, first, just in case it was not OK? But the servants just did as Jesus told them, and poured some into the master's cup. I held my breath and could not look away as he lifted the drink to his lips. I saw it all in slow motion. He swallowed, put his cup down, wiped his lips and then beckoned to the bridegroom. The two of them moved apart from everyone else and were soon deep in conversation. I was so worried; the drink must have been awful. Would Jesus be in trouble?

But I needn't have been concerned. I soon saw the master and bridegroom drinking some more and smiling and laughing together. It turns out that the master had been confused because the wine tasted so good! He was asking the bridegroom why he had saved the best till last, since most people use the best wine first.

I was so relieved, and it wasn't until I sat down (drink in hand) that I stopped to think about what had actually happened. Jesus – my son – had turned water into wine.

Here we have a wedding day problem (John 2:1–11).
So Mary turns to Jesus and asks him to fix it.
Which he does.

Seems simple enough . . . but wait.
Why did Mary think Jesus would be able to perform such a miracle?
It's not as though he had done anything like this before.
She had not seen him perform any miracles.
She wasn't thinking he would just do what he always did –

because he had *never done this before.*

Well, Mary might not have seen Jesus fix a problem in this way before, but she had *lived* with him for thirty years.
She had spent time with him.
She had got to know him.
And so, even though she had never seen him perform a miracle before, because she knew him, because she had shared her life with him, she had learned to trust him.

Mary had learned through being with Jesus that he was someone who was able to do more than she expected, more than she hoped for, more than she even looked for.

Ephesians 3:20:
'[God] is able to do immeasurably more than all we ask or imagine, according to his power . . . at work within us'.

What about you?

Your God is a God who can do immeasurably more.

But is your God also a God who is limited by your doubts?
By your fears?
By your uncertainties?
By your lack of trust?

How about following Mary's example –
when you don't know what to do,

when the way ahead seems uncertain,
when the problem seems insurmountable . . . turn to
Jesus.
And leave it with him.

And then wait and see what he does.
Give him a chance . . . and see water turn into wine.
See problems turn into solutions.
See fear turn into reassurance.
See doubt turn into joy.

God is a God of water-into-wine moments – don't miss
out on the wine because you are too scared to mention
the water to him.

And don't forget to trust him.

Imagine the trust it took from those servants to pour
out water for the master of the banquet!
But they did it.
Because Jesus had told them to.
Despite the lack of evidence, they did it.

They trusted Jesus, picked up water and poured out
wine.

Imagine what God can do with what you've got.
With your possessions, with your relationships, with
your time.

So, give it all to him.
Then pick it up, pour it out . . . and watch for a water-into-wine moment.

Lord God,

You are amazing.
Thank you that you take what I offer, what I have, what I am and turn it into something extra special.
Sometimes I find it hard to believe – but I know you can do it.
Help me to give you what I have, and to leave it with you.
To let you deal with it.
Help me to see the water-into-wine moments.

Amen

Mary's memo

See water change to wine

My response:

Day 28

I have had a terrible day. Jesus has been so busy recently, I have hardly seen him at all. Crowds follow him everywhere he goes. They want to listen to him, see him do miracles, spend time with him, just see him . . . Today I heard that people were surrounding him so much that even in a house, he was unable to eat! Something inside me snapped. This is just too much – Jesus is still 'my baby' and I hate to think of him exhausting himself like this. I mentioned it to some of the rest of the family and they agreed. So we went to the house where Jesus was not eating. When we got there, surprise, surprise, we could not get into the house. There were people everywhere! So we thought that the best thing to do was to ask someone to go and tell Jesus that we were there and were looking for him.

We waited outside and eventually we saw the man who had gone to get Jesus. He was pushing his way towards us through the crowd – and he was alone. Where was Jesus?

The man seemed reluctant to tell us exactly what had been said, but I insisted – and then wished that I hadn't. Jesus had said, 'Who are my mother and brothers?'

Now, that hurt. Was he rejecting us?

Apparently, he had gone on to say that whoever does God's will is his mother and brother and sister.

I have to confess that I did not stick around. Tears were blurring my vision and I had to get away from there. Was Jesus rejecting us? Rejecting me?

This story is found in Mark 3:20,21,31–35.
Mary has not had a great day – and we can see why she is feeling upset – but let's take a closer look and see what we can learn from what happened:

Mary and her family are looking for Jesus.
They know where he is, they want to find him, but they just can't quite get to him.

So, what do they do?

They ask someone to help.
They don't try to fight their way through the crowd, through the obstacles, on their own – they ask for help.

What about you?
Are you looking for Jesus?
Maybe for the first time.
Maybe trying to find him in a given situation.
Maybe you've lost sight of him . . .
You know where he is, you want to reach him, but you're finding that you just can't quite get to him?

Maybe you need to follow Mary's example and ask someone for help. Don't be too proud. Ask someone to talk with you, pray with you – and help you get through to Jesus again.

The reason why Mary was having difficulty doing what she wanted to do was because of the crowd. They were frustrating. They were in the way.

But they had every right to be there.

They were like Mary – they just wanted to be near Jesus. And that was fine with Jesus.
They were all welcome – and Mary needed to realize that.

Sometimes, let's be honest, church life can be frustrating.
People annoy us.
People get in the way of how we want to do things.

But we need to remember what we have in common – we all want to be near Jesus. And we are all welcome (see Luke 9:11). We are in his family:

Psalm 133:1:
'How good and pleasant it is when brothers live together in unity!'

Let's try it!

It must have been hard for Mary when the messenger came back and reported that Jesus had asked, 'Who are my mother and brothers?'
Why would Jesus say something like that?

Maybe he was making the point that when it comes to God's family, all are equal. He wasn't rejecting Mary as his human mother; he was accepting everyone in his spiritual family as equal to her in value.

Mary had to realize that her son embraced and loved the whole crowd, the whole world, even . . . but, importantly, it did not mean that he loved her any less (we will see tomorrow just how much he loved her).

It is possible to look at other Christians, and start making comparisons between you and them. They seem happier, more fulfilled, more blessed than you.

And you are going through a hard time,
struggling to get to Jesus,
stuck on the edge of the crowd.

And that's tough.
It is hard.
But it does not mean that God loves you less than them.
It does not mean that he loves them more than you.

John 3:16:
'God so loved the world . . .'

And 'the world' means everyone – including you.
God has such an amazing capacity to love.
And he does not make comparisons.
Love is who he is.
And he gives you his love, 100 per cent:

Isaiah 43:3,4:
*'I am . . . your God . . . you are precious and
honoured in my sight, and . . . I love you '.*

Lord God,

I do make comparisons, I admit it.
Help me to remember that I don't need to.
I don't need to because you don't.
And Lord, sometimes I find other people hard.
They annoy me, if I am honest.
Help me to love them as you love them,
To embrace them as members of your family.

Amen

Mary's memo

Love God's family

My response:

Day 29

My heart is breaking. Today I saw my Jesus nailed
to a cross, lifted up high and left to die. My son –
the one who crowds follow, who does miracles, who
heals the sick. My son – left to die in front of a
mocking crowd, all watching him like vultures.
My son – who has been falsely accused and is the
victim of a conspiracy. My son – who, to me, is still
the baby I cradled all those years ago; who I played
with and laughed with. My son – left hanging on
a cross between two thieves. The thieves were dying
for their crimes, but what about Jesus? He hasn't ever
done anything wrong. How is this fair? And then,
he spoke. From the cross. When he was nearly dead,
through the most horrendous pain, I heard his voice.
Jesus was speaking, and he was speaking directly to
me. I didn't think I had this many tears inside me.
Jesus told me that John, one of his closest friends,
would take care of me now. Jesus was going through
the most agonizing thing, and yet he thought of me.
He knew I'd be lost without him, so he gave me John.
Not long after that, Jesus died.

Then Nicodemus arrived – he used to be a secret
follower of Jesus, but I guess he isn't secret any more,
because he openly asked for Jesus' body. Then he and

a friend buried Jesus in a brand new tomb. I am so grateful, and I hope Nicodemus knows it – my boy deserves the best, but I have been too upset to say anything much to anyone.

The Romans rolled a stone over the front of the tomb and then, believe it or not, the priests placed a guard outside the tomb as well. Something about them being worried that someone would steal the body and claim Jesus rose from the dead. But they can do what they want. Jesus is dead and something in me died along with him. I can't write any more now . . .

Jesus hangs on a cross.
The crowd shout.
The sky turns black.
Mary weeps.
Her son dies.

But why? Why did Jesus have to die?

See Isaiah 53:4–6:

You turned your back on him and looked the other way.
He was despised, and you did not care.
Yet it was your weaknesses he carried;
it was your sorrows that weighed him down . . .
Jesus was beaten so you could be whole.
He was whipped so you could be healed.

You're like a sheep, you have strayed away.
You have left God's paths to follow your own.
Yet the L<small>ORD</small> laid on Jesus
every single one of your sins.

So you could be whole.

That's why Jesus died.
He did it for you.
So, every time you feel
broken,
useless,
a failure,
worthless . . .

Remember that you are worth it to Jesus.

You are worth dying for.

You are worth making whole.

And every time you turn your back on him, even for a
moment . . .
Remember that you are still worth it.
He still died for you.
He can still bring you back.
He can still make you whole.

Remember the verse we looked at on Day 18 –

Zephaniah 3:17:
'The LORD your God is with you,
he is mighty to save.
He will take great delight in you,
he will quiet you with his love,
he will rejoice over you with singing.'

Jesus delights in you, and you are his joy.

Next time you think that no one cares,
that no one wants you,
that you are boring,
remind yourself:

Jesus rejoices in me. Full stop.

But does he rejoice in what you say?
Does he rejoice in what you do?

Every day is a chance to give Jesus joy.
Every day is full of 'joy opportunities'.
Opportunities to live his way.
Opportunities that will make him smile.

Will you take them?

Day 29

Lord God,

I don't get it.
I give you joy? I am worth dying for?
Wow. I can't understand it.
Please help me to know that you accept me.
That you accept me because of Jesus.
I want to accept your joy.
And I want to give joy back to you.

Amen

Mary's memo

Look for joy

My response:

Day 30

Is it really him? Jesus? I thought I saw him. I hope I saw him. It certainly looks like him . . . it is him. Jesus is alive again!

And it is definitely not my imagination: other people have seen him, too.

I am an emotional wreck right now. A few days ago, I was watching Jesus die, and now I have just had a conversation with him. And it was a normal conversation – he is definitely alive!

I've just flicked back through my diary, and it is amazing how far I've come. I was only 14 when I started keeping this record; it's hard to believe that over thirty years have passed since then.

On the first page I wrote the things that were important about me. It makes me laugh to read them now – favourite colour, hair colour etc. . . . If only I had been able to see what was coming, I'm sure that my favourite colour would have been the last thing on my mind.

An angel coming, being bullied, travelling to Bethlehem (while nine months pregnant), giving birth to Jesus, being visited by shepherds and wise men, losing Jesus in the Temple, seeing Jesus turn water into wine, seeing Jesus die on a cross, seeing

Jesus alive again, plus all the things that happened that I did not have time to write about . . . no, favourite colour would definitely not make the list.

Which makes me think, what <u>would</u> make the list?

Mmmm, it's really hard to sum it up, and I think that is because everything on the list involves Jesus –

My name is Mary . . . and I am Jesus' mother. I am Jesus' friend. I have seen Jesus do miracles. I know what Jesus likes to eat . . . You see? I would be here forever if I continue this list. I think I am finding this hard because since Jesus was born, my life has become more and more wrapped up in him and who he is.

So it is really difficult to write a list of things that are important about me now . . . but I think I know how to sum it up in one sentence:

My name is Mary, and I know Jesus.

'Jesus is alive!'

Mary has been on quite a journey.

She brought Jesus into the world and now, thirty-three years later, having seen him die, having thought he was dead, she has the joy of knowing that he is alive.

That she can continue to know him, talk with him, see him . . .

that she can continue her life with him.

She has come from a place where Jesus did not even exist to a place where she cannot imagine life without him.

Because life is so much better when Jesus is around.
Did you know that?
Do you know that?
Jesus is alive – and he wants to share that life with *you*.
He wants you to know that difficult times with him are better than easy times without him.
He wants you to realize that knowing yourself is less important than being known by him.
He wants you to come to a place of abundant life – and all through knowing him.

John 10:10 (NKJV):
Jesus said, 'I have come that [you] may have life, and . . . have it . . . abundantly.'

What about your journey?
How is it going?
Is it full of life?

Because it can be.

You can come to a place of abundant life, again and again, and all through knowing Jesus.

Lord God,

Thank you, thank you, thank you . . .

Amen

Mary's memo

Jesus; know him
and live

My response:

Milton Keynes UK
Ingram Content Group UK Ltd.
UKHW021810241123
433186UK00010B/347

9 781860 249358